A Rebel's Guide to George Orwell

ACKNOWLEDGEMENTS
I would like to thank Colm Bryce and Simon Assaf for their work
on the production of this book. Also special thanks to my partner
Lorna Chessum who will be quite happy to never hear George
Orwell's name ever again

ABOUT THE AUTHOR
John Newsinger is the author of two books about George Orwell
Orwell's Politics (1999) and *Hope Lies in the Proles: George Orwell
and the Left* (2018) as well as a large number of other books
including the best-selling *The Blood Never Dried: A People's
History of the British Empire* (2006).

COVER IMAGE: Orwell at his flat at 27b Canonbury Square
in Islington, late 1946. Photograph: Vernon Richards
INSIDE FRONT: Orwell with the POUM militia on the
Aragon Front during the Spanish Civil War in 1937.
Photograph: Christopher Thomond
INSIDE BACK: Orwell late 1946. Photograph: Vernon Richards

Published by Bookmarks Publications 2020
Copyright Bookmarks, 1 Bloomsbury Street, London WC1B 3QE
ISBN print edition: 978-1-914143-00-7
ISBN Kindle: 978-1-914143-01-4
ISBN ePub: 978-1-914143-02-1
ISBN PDF: 978-1-914143-03-8

Series design by Noel Douglas
Typeset by Simon Assaf for Bookmarks Publications
Printed by Halstan & Co Ltd, Amersham, Buckinghamshire,
England

A Rebel's Guide to
ORWELL

JOHN NEWSINGER

ALSO IN THIS SERIES:
A Rebel's Guide to James Connolly by Sean Mitchell
A Rebel's Guide to Eleanor Marx by Siobhan Brown
A Rebel's Guide to Rosa Luxemburg by Sally Campbell
A Rebel's Guide to Gramsci by Chris Bambery
A Rebel's Guide to Trotsky by Esme Choonara
A Rebel's Guide to Marx by Mike Gonzalez
A Rebel's Guide to Lenin by Ian Birchall
A Rebel's Guide to Malcolm X by Antony Hamilton
A Rebel's Guide to Martin Luther King by Yuri Prasad
A Rebel's Guide to Alexandra Kollontai by Emma Davis
A Rebel's Guide to Friedrich Engels by Camilla Royle
Sexism and the System: A Rebel's Guide to Women's Liberation
    by Judith Orr
Available from Bookmarks, 1 Bloomsbury Street, London WC1B 3QE
www.bookmarksbookshop.co.uk ı 020 7637 1848

★ 1: INTRODUCTION

George Orwell died in January 1950, aged only 46 years of age. He was best known as a socialist novelist and journalist, the author of a book about mass unemployment in the North of England, *The Road to Wigan Pier*, of a book about revolutionary Barcelona in 1937, *Homage to Catalonia*, one of the very few sympathetic first-hand accounts of a revolution by a British participant and observer, and of two ferociously anti-Stalinist novels, *Animal Farm* and *Nineteen Eighty Four*. Both *Animal Farm* and *Nineteen Eighty Four* were hijacked, indeed weaponised, for use in the Cold War after his premature death. Interest in his other writings continued throughout the 1950s and into the 1960s so that he never became a mere literary footnote like so many other writers. And then in the late 1960s with the opposition to the Vietnam War, the widespread disillusionment with the Wilson Labour government, indeed with Labourism more generally, and with the growth of student radicalism his socialist politics were rediscovered. More recently, however, interest in George Orwell has positively soared. Why is this?

It is very much in response to the times we live in: people are turning to Orwell's writings because of contemporary developments, looking for both answers and inspiration. There is the harsh impact of austerity regimes on millions of people, both in 'Food Bank' Britain and abroad. The poverty and hunger, the job insecurity and deteriorating working conditions, the worsening housing conditions and increase in homelessness, all the miseries that are part of everyday life for millions of people in Britain today, give Orwell a very contemporary relevance. The savage cutback of social provision, whether it be in housing, schooling, health or benefits, is all part of a deliberate, yes deliberate, sustained attack on the working class for the benefit of big business and the rich. And all this has been accompanied by the continuing drive to privatise everything that can make a profit for big business, whether it be done openly, like the Royal Mail (courtesy of Liberal Democrat Vince Cable it is worth remembering) or by stealth, piece by piece, like in education and the NHS. This attack on many fronts, class war from above, has been grinding people down remorselessly since the 1980s, starting with Thatcher, consolidated under Blair and Brown and then relentlessly intensified under Cameron, May and Johnson. We actually have a situation in Britain today, one of the richest countries in the world, where children are going hungry and where the government's housing policy for millions of people is, in practical terms, a return to the slum housing of the past despite all their empty rhetoric about home ownership. What we have to recognise is that it is not that the system isn't working. It is working all too well… for the benefit of the rich and super rich. While the May government actually boasted of creating a 'hostile environment' for immigrants, and the racist treatment of the 'Windrush Generation' is certainly one of the most shameful episodes of recent times, May has, in fact, created a 'hostile environment' for everyone who is not rich. Orwell would have had no trouble recognising this attack for what it is. This is why *The Road to Wigan Pier*, more than eighty years after its publication, still resonates, still speaks to us today.

And there is more. There is the increasing levels of surveillance, both government and corporate, just about everywhere, from the USA to China and places in between. Facebook, it turns out, is a close relative of Big Brother. Indeed, we live in a world increasingly dominated by billionaire Big Brother oligarchs. We are also experiencing a dramatic increase in routine everyday dishonesty on the part of politicians and governments, something not unrelated to the dominance of the new class of the super rich. Politicians have always lied, but have never been so unconcerned at being caught in the lie. This has been compounded by the brazen denial of known facts and championing of 'alternative facts' by the Trump administration in the United States. Orwell's 2+2=5 if that's what the government wants scenario from *Nineteen Eighty Four* seems to be, indeed actually is, the official position of President Trump and his courtiers. The consequences of all this when global warming threatens the whole planet are going to be truly catastrophic. Alongside this there is the rise of the far right, the revival of racism and fascism and the spread of authoritarianism across much of the world. This is how ruling classes have always sustained themselves in power at times of crisis: turn ordinary people against each other, get them to blame each other for society's ills rather than turn on those really responsible, big business, the bankers, the rich and the super rich. A saviour will emerge in the shape of a right-wing authoritarian ruler with dictatorial ambitions and at least some of the trappings of fascism.

All these developments have led many people to

look to Orwell for help in understanding our times. Consequently, it is of great importance to know exactly what Orwell stood for, what were the causes that he spent his life fighting for, what were his strengths, what were his weaknesses and, of course, to rescue him from those who seek to domesticate him, to eliminate from his biography his fierce commitment to the establishment of a classless socialist system throughout the world. A good example of this attempted domestication is the statue to Orwell put up outside the BBC. Orwell, of course, had worked as a propagandist at the BBC during the Second World War, but he had no illusions as to the nature of the organisation and its chosen role. As he observed at the end of the War, the BBC still had "the same subtly reactionary colour it always had" *(Complete Works 17, p 417)*. Nothing new there then! Moreover, the sheer hypocrisy of the BBC trying to embrace Orwell, to make use of his reputation, is demonstrated by the certain fact that no one espousing his political opinions would ever get a job at the Corporation today. But what were his political beliefs? As well as exposing the appalling living and working conditions experienced by working class people in the 1930s and opposing totalitarian police dictatorships whether fascist or communist in the 1940s, Orwell was also a champion of working class revolution. He had been a witness to and participant in revolution in Barcelona in 1937, an experience that changed his life, and left him convinced right up until his death in January 1950 that it was 'the proles', the working class, who were the agency of change and who would bring about the socialist revolution and the classless socialist society he hoped for.

2:
THE BRITISH
EMPIRE OR THE
POX BRITANNICA

Eric Blair (he only assumed the pseudonym George Orwell for literary purposes with the publication of *Down and Out in Paris and London* in 1933) was very much a child of Empire. He had been born on 25 June 1903 in India where his father worked in the government's opium department. Admirers of British imperialism will assume that he was involved in suppressing the use of the drug, but those less naïve will not be surprised that his job was in producing and marketing a very lucrative export to China. It had taken three bloody wars, including the military occupation of Beijing, to force the Chinese to open their country to Britain's government-backed drug pushers. As was very much the custom at the time, young Eric returned to Britain for his education, going to a preparatory school and then on to Eton, the privileged establishment where the country's rulers were and, of course, still are prepared for the exercise of power, born to rule. He later described it as "the most costly and snobbish of the English public schools" (CW 19, p 86). He was a scholarship boy and subsequently claimed to have already had rebellious ideas even at Eton, but his choice of career shows that, such tendencies were, at the very least, temporarily suppressed. In 1922, he joined the Indian police as an officer cadet and was sent out

6

to help control Burma (modern day Myanmar) for the Empire.

While Orwell (as we shall call him from now on) was an avid reader and his political development was always to be informed by what he read and the discussions and arguments that resulted from his reading, it is also important to remember that personal experience was absolutely vital. This was particularly true with regard to his experiences in Burma. Here whatever the naïve expectations he might have had when he arrived in the country, he found himself part of "the actual machinery of despotism", keeping the Burmese people down by brute force so they could be ruthlessly exploited by British capitalists. Over time he came to have "an indescribable loathing" for the imperial system, later recalling "the wretched prisoners squatting in the reeking cages of the lock-ups... the scarred buttocks of the men who had been flogged with bamboos... things like these are beyond bearing when you are in any way directly responsible for them". He saw "the dirty work of Empire at close quarters" and ended up hating "the imperialism I was serving with a bitterness I can probably not make clear" (*The Road to Wigan Pier*, pp 127-130).

In his first novel, *Burmese Days*, that was to be published in 1935, the main character, Flory, speaks for Orwell when he argues that the proper name for the British Empire was 'Pox Britannica'. The reason the British were in Burma was not to further any humanitarian civilising mission, but "to steal. It's so simple. The official holds the Burman down while the businessman goes through his pockets". Flory points out that before the British conquered India the country had had its own industrial base, shipbuilding for example, but the British had shut it all down, "crushed various industries". And did anyone imagine that the firm he worked for would get timber contracts "if the country weren't in the hands of the British"? Of course not. Indeed, Flory's disgust at the realities of imperialism is such that he actually finds himself longing "for a native rising to drown their Empire in blood" (*Burmese Days*, pp 36-43).

Orwell not only came to hate the Empire for what it was doing to the Burmese, but also for what it was doing to him. As he later recalled, he got into the habit of striking servants for such minor offences as spilling a drink, being too slow to obey instructions. Nearly everyone did this. It was the routine currency of social interaction between the colonised and the coloniser. Much later, he was to consider the essential part that racism played in justifying all this. It was, as he put it, one of "the necessary props of imperialism". He went on: "You can only rule over a subject race, especially when you are in a small minority, if you honestly believe yourself to be racially superior" (CW 16, p 435).

Orwell had to get out. He resigned from the Burmese police while on leave in England in the autumn of 1927. He had returned home, as he later put it, "with a bad conscience", "haunted intolerably" by "remembered faces – faces of prisoners in the dock… of subordinates I had bullied… of servants... I had hit with my fist in moments of rage… I was conscious of an immense weight of guilt that I had got to expiate". He came home, not only a bitter opponent of British imperialism, but of "every form of man's dominion over man. I wanted to submerge myself, to get right down among the oppressed, to be one of them, and on their side against their tyrants" (Wigan Pier, pp 129-130).

On his way home from Burma, he stopped off in Marseilles and for the very first time saw the working class in action, on the streets, protesting against injustice. He was standing outside a bank when "an immense procession of working people streamed past, bearing banners inscribed 'Sauvons Sacco et Vanzetti' ['Save Sacco and Vanzetti', two Italian immigrant anarchists, framed for murder and sentenced to death in the United States]… All these people – tens of thousands of them – were genuinely indignant over a piece of injustice, and thought it quite natural to lose a day's wages in order to say so". In France, when French workers talked about 'la revolution', he observed, they meant "the next revolution, not the last one" (CW 10, pp244-245).

★ 3:
THE WORKING CLASS ON THE DEFENSIVE

I n the Britain Orwell came home to, the working class had just suffered an historic defeat at the hands of the Conservative government. The miners had been locked out for refusing to accept pay cuts and longer hours in May 1926 and the TUC had called a General Strike in their support. This unprecedented display of working class solidarity was getting stronger by the day. When it was called off after nine days, many workers assumed they had won. All over the country, there was stunned incredulity when the enormity of the betrayal by the union leadership became clear. The TUC leadership was terrified of the struggle getting out of hand and called it off without even securing no-victim-isation agreements for the men and women they had called out on strike. Not only were over a million miners left to fight on alone, but thousands of the workers who had come out in their support were victimised or found their wages cut and their unions de-recognised. The *Guardian* newspaper, for example, imposed a company union on its printers. The miners stayed out for another six months before being driven back to work by hunger, police repression and the setting up of scab unions. Many miners were victimised for their part in the struggle, blacklisted and driven out of the industry. This was a great historic defeat for the whole working class. Orwell was still in Burma when the General Strike and Miners' Lockout took place, but he was back home for the next great betrayal.

In May 1929, the Labour Party won the largest number of seats of any party in the Commons and Ramsay Macdonald formed the second Labour government. Confronted with the onset of the Great Depression, Labour did not use the great crisis of capitalism to begin overthrowing the system. Instead, they set about trying to solve the crisis at the expense of the working class, of their own supporters. When Labour took office there were 1,164,000 unemployed, by June 1931 the number had risen to 2,700,000 and was getting worse by the day. The government's answer was to cut the dole and, at the same time, to disqualify as many of the unemployed as possible from claiming it, and to cut the pay of public sector workers including teachers, civil servants and the armed forces. The Cabinet was divided, not over the cuts mind; they had all agreed cuts had to be made, but over their severity. This was not good enough for Macdonald who broke away to establish a Tory-dominated coalition, the National Government, that forced the full cuts through. The Labour Party saw its number of MPs reduced from 289 before the 1931 general election to 46 afterwards. This was the political and social context that Orwell encountered when he returned to Britain. The working class had suffered massive defeats on a scale that was not to be repeated until the mid-1980s. The unions had been seriously weakened, there was mass unemployment and a Labour government had shown a readiness to put the interests of the bankers before the interests of the working class.

What of Orwell? He had two concerns at this time: to expiate the profound guilt he felt about his time in Burma and to become a writer. He was determined to experience life as it was lived by the most oppressed men and women in Britain, the homeless casual labourers, the 'down and outs', tramping the country, looking for work. His first such expedition was in late 1927 and he had his great moment of epiphany when, dressed as a 'tramp', a working class man called him 'mate'! He was to carry out further expeditions living among the homeless poor in 1930 and 1931. He described how they were routinely bullied, humiliated, left without any self-respect, treated 'like cattle', but, as he insisted, the 'down and outs' were just people ground down by poverty and insecurity. As far as he was concerned the only difference between the homeless and the middle class was money. Only fifteen years ago, his account would have seemed to be of merely historic or literary interest, but today, with the number of the homeless and the hungry still relentlessly rising as a deliberate consequence of the Tory government's austerity regime, once again sacrificing ordinary people, men, women and children, for the benefit of the bankers, it has a painfully contemporary resonance.

Orwell went to live in Paris in order to write. It was here that he first got involved with the Left, writing for French socialist newspapers on the condition of the British working class and about British imperialism. He also wrote to the *Workers' Weekly*, the British Communist Party newspaper, offering to become their Paris correspondent. It was this that first brought him to the attention of MI5 who presumably intercepted his letter and had a report prepared on this former colonial policeman who was defecting to the Left. Nothing came of his offer to write for the *Workers' Weekly* (published until 1939).

While he was certainly already on the left, his two priorities at this time were still experiencing life as it was lived by the poor and becoming a writer. On his return home from France, he once again went on the tramp, before turning his experiences in France and Britain into his book *Down and Out in Paris and London*. The book was not published until 1933.

★ 4: WIGAN

Orwell never considered joining the Labour Party at this time. There was not only the Labour government's betrayal of the unemployed, but while in office the government had also brutally repressed the Congress movement's campaign of civil disobedience in India. Protestors were shot down in the street, publicly flogged and even hanged. The Labour government imprisoned some 60,000 people including Mahatma Gandhi, the independence movement's leader. And, it was while Labour were in power that the Saya San peasant rebellion broke out in Burma between 1930 and 1932, and was eventually put down with some 3,000 rebels killed and wounded, 8,000 imprisoned and over 120 executed. In at least one district, the heads of dead rebels were displayed on poles. The government's shameful performance, both at home and in the colonies, had provoked the breakaway of a socialist affiliate to the Labour Party, one of the organisations that had helped establish it, the Independent Labour Party (ILP). In March 1932, the ILP voted to disaffiliate from the Labour Party and it was towards this organisation that Orwell was drawn. He became involved with the *Adelphi* magazine, edited by John Middleton Murray. It was, to all intents and purposes, the ILP's theoretical magazine and he was very influenced by its concern with working class life and experience and by its leftist politics.

It was his concern with working class life that led

the left-wing publisher, Victor Gollancz, to commission Orwell to write what was to become *The Road to Wigan Pier*. Orwell was sent to the north of England to report on the condition of the working class. While the Midlands and the South-East were beginning to recover from the Great Depression, although there was still considerable poverty, low wages, bad housing and great hardship, in the North there was still the scourge of mass unemployment. Orwell set about telling a middle class left-wing readership how bad things still were and then went on to consider why there was no great working class revolt against such conditions, why it was that people put up with it all.

The Road to Wigan Pier is best read alongside the diary that Orwell kept during his time in the North. The diary records his day to day activities, the help he received during his investigations from working class socialists and communists, whereas the book was written very much as a work of propaganda and polemic. What he saw in the North was the consequences of working class defeat. He celebrated the miners, the work they did and its importance to society. One in every 900 miners died in an industrial accident every year with many more suffering serious injury. Mining was the most dangerous job in Britain and yet instead of being celebrated and rewarded for doing such dangerous essential work, they had been demonised by the media, attacked by the government and coal companies and reduced to conditions of virtual serfdom. His concern in the book was to chronicle their oppression and exploitation, but even when he arrived in the North, the fight back was already beginning. In November 1935, the Miners'

Federation had balloted for national strike action and had won a 97 percent vote in favour. Only an improved pay offer from the coal companies averted a strike. But for that improved offer, Orwell would have arrived in the North to find the miners on strike, the pits shut down and picketed with the inevitable clashes with the police and scabs. *The Road to Wigan Pier* would have been a very different book, a book celebrating struggle rather than a book intent on exposing hardship, a book advocating solidarity rather than one intended to evoke sympathy.

He went on to chronicle the appalling housing conditions he found, describing, for example, the miserable caravan colonies that many working class families were forced to live in. One thing that surprised him was that so few people were rude or unhelpful when he enquired about their hardships. Only one woman told him to push off and he thought she had misheard him because she was deaf and thought he was collecting the rates. And then there was unemployment. There were still some two million people officially unemployed but, as he pointed out, there were more people not registered. On top of that many people were underemployed. Orwell actually describes in 1936 the demoralising impact of increasing casualisation on the working class and the way that this was welcomed and celebrated by some ruling class apologists as a way of disciplining the working class, keeping them subordinate. He singled out a certain Professor Saintsbury as one such "skunk". Orwell would have no trouble recognising the 'zero hours' contract and agency work for what it is today! He saw its equivalent in the 1930s. If you counted the unemployed, both registered and unregistered, the underemployed, and all their dependents that meant some ten million people were living in poverty and hardship, hungry, ill-clothed and badly housed in slum conditions.

Orwell praised what he saw of the activities of the Communist-led National Unemployed Workers' Movement (NUWM). As he put it, he "greatly admired" the NUWM activists who were intent on building "a revolutionary organisation intended to hold the working class together". They urged the unemployed to support workers in struggle by refusing to scab and reinforcing them on the picket line. But it was always an uphill struggle. He was depressed by what he saw as the lack of fight back. People were adapting to, making the best of their circumstances, rather than trying to change them by mass action. After he had attended a meeting in Wigan in support of Ernst Thaelmann, the leader of the German Communist Party, imprisoned by the Nazis, he recorded that if this was the best the revolutionary left could do then "God help us... There is no turbulence left in England". He acknowledged how people were relentlessly ground down by hardship, pressed "into a passive role". They did not act, but rather were "acted upon" (CW 10, p 431). This was, of course, hardly surprising after the defeat of the General Strike and Miners' Lockout only ten years earlier and the betrayals of the Labour government only five years before.

He also went to a meeting called by the British Union of Fascists, Oswald Mosley's Blackshirts, in Barnsley. There were some 700 people in the audience, listening to "the usual claptrap… down with the Jew and the foreigner". Mosley blamed everything on "international gangs of Jews". As he later told his friend, the working class writer Jack Common, Mosley talked complete "bollix" and he very much doubted that he actually believed any of it himself. A number of hecklers were beaten up by the Blackshirt stewards and then handed over to the police and arrested. The cooperation that he witnessed between the fascists and the police was something that still infuriated him ten years later. As far as Orwell was concerned though, Mosley was not a serious threat. The real fascist threat in Britain, when it came and he was certain it was coming, would manifest itself in a "slimy Anglicised form" and would certainly not call itself fascist (CW 10, pp 456-457). It would wear the colours of British nationalism rather than be a poor copy of the Italian and German movements.

One last point is worth making here: Orwell's activities in the North once again brought him to the attention of MI5. An extremely perceptive member of Special Branch sent to investigate his activities reported back to his superiors that he was probably an author: "As he devotes most of his time to writing".

★5: MIDDLE CLASS FADDISM

The second half of *The Road to Wigan Pier*, where Orwell provides a jaundiced, idiosyncratic and wholly unbalanced survey of the British Left is the most controversial part of the book. Although it was to be published by the Left Book Club and was, indeed, its best selling title, Gollancz felt it necessary to distance himself from the volume with an apologetic Introduction. In *The Road to Wigan Pier*, Orwell not only succeeded in alienating the Communist Party by disparaging their worship of the Soviet Union and criticising the politics of the Popular Front, but he also attacked those middle class socialists within the ILP who, he felt, were putting working class people off the socialist cause.

As far as he was concerned, it was obvious that socialism was the necessary solution to the world's problems, the only answer to the dangers that threatened. And he did not mean a Labour government, but "Socialism as a world-system and wholeheartedly applied". As far as the Labourite Fabians were concerned socialism was a package of reforms to be imposed on the working class for their own good, rather than a mass movement of the working class to overthrow capitalism.

But what of the ILP? Its middle class members with their vegetarianism, feminism, nudism, pacifism and obsession with sexual liberation, walking around in shorts and sandals and drinking fruit juice were driving working class men and women away. One dreads to think how he would have responded to veganism! They were all "faddists" and they had turned socialism into a "fad". This was, to use his own words against him, just so much "bollix". More generally, the failure of a fight back to develop in Britain in the late 1930s, such as took place in France, Spain and in the United States, cannot be seriously blamed on a small number of middle class socialists in the ILP, no matter how annoying Orwell found them. It was a consequence of historic defeats. Nevertheless, whatever its weaknesses, he still saw the ILP as the most promising organisation on the left, as the place where the building of a mass socialist movement that actually meant business could begin. The fascist menace, both in Britain and abroad, made the task all the more urgent.

It is worth noticing here that Orwell's hostility to feminism reflected his generally sexist attitudes and occasional behaviour towards women. This sexism persisted despite his being married to a very strong independent woman, Eileen, and having women friends who were determined feminists. A good example of one of these friends is Ethel Mannin, an ILP member, who published her tremendous *Women and the Revolution* in 1938, a book which Orwell never seems to have read. And, moreover, as she chronicles in that book, the fight for women's liberation was very much part of the Spanish Revolution that Orwell was soon on his way to fight for. He remained throughout his life one of those male socialists opposed to all oppression...except that of women.

★6:
THE SPANISH
REVOLUTION

The coming to power of an elected Popular Front government in Spain, a government committed to a programme of radical reform, provoked a right-wing military coup on 17-18 July 1936. The coup failed. Instead of the government being overthrown, with some shooting on the streets, the summary execution of troublemakers and mass arrests, the working class rose up in revolt. The coup was intended to prevent a programme of reform but instead provoked a full-blown revolution. The working class, led by the mass anarchist trade union the CNT (Confederación Nacional del Trabajo or National Confederation of Labour), took to the streets, in city after city, town after town, defeating the army and taking control. Revolutionary committees were set up, and factories, shops, transport and farms were seized by the workers and peasants. A state of dual power had been established in much of Republican Spain, for the first time in Europe since the revolutionary wave that had been unleashed by the Russian Revolution. These revolutionary committees did not move to overthrow the Popular Front government and establish workers' power, however, but rather gave it their support, not least because while the military coup had failed, the Spanish Army under General Franco had, with German and Italian backing, plunged the country into a bloody civil war.

All across Europe and beyond, militants and activists, men and women, determined to go to Spain to fight against the Spanish military and their fascist allies. Orwell was one of them. The Communist International took the lead in organising these volunteers into the International Brigades and Orwell initially applied to join the British contingent. He was turned down because of his public criticisms of Communism, and so instead joined the ILP contingent that went out to join the radical socialist POUM militia in Barcelona. This was a one of the decisive moments in his biography. Although Orwell always acknowledged that the International Brigade volunteers were brave idealists, fighting and dying to hold back the advance of fascism – indeed one in four of them were to die in the fighting – there was another dimension to the movement that should not, indeed must not be forgotten.

The Communist International was wholly controlled by the Stalin regime in the Soviet Union and although it used the rhetoric of socialism and solidarity, in practice it acted in the interests of the Soviet Union as a great power. The Soviet Union, it has to be insisted, had no sentimental attachment whatever to the cause of the international working class at this time, indeed between 1933 and 1935 it had been allied with Fascist Italy and between 1939 and 1941 it was to be allied with Nazi Germany. The only interest Stalin had in Spain was in preventing the country falling into the hands of a military dictatorship allied with Germany and Italy who he saw as a threat at that moment. He hoped to ally with France and Britain against this threat. This foreign policy objective meant that it was vital that the revolutionary movement in Spain be rolled back in case it should scare off the British and French.

So much is generally acknowledged today. But there

was another motive behind the counter-revolutionary role that the Communist International was to play in Spain. The establishment of a genuine democratic workers' state in Spain would have inevitably posed a mortal threat to the Stalin regime, exposing it as a brutal, murderous dictatorship. Stalin headed up a dictatorship that had at that time imprisoned and executed considerably more Communists than the Nazis had and that had moreover subjected the Russian working class to a modern serfdom with millions sent to the slave labour camps where many of them were worked to death. Seeing a genuine workers' state in action would lead to Communist Party members throughout the world questioning their allegiance to the Stalin dictatorship and might even focus unrest in the Soviet Union itself. The Spanish Revolution had to be rolled back and the revolutionary left had to be discredited and destroyed by whatever methods were necessary.

Excluded from the International Brigades, Orwell travelled to Barcelona where he joined the ILP contingent in the POUM militia. The POUM (Partido Obrero de Unificación Marxista or Workers' Party of Marxist Unification), was a revolutionary organisation that included in its ranks and leadership former Trotskyists. It supported the Popular Front government, but urged that the revolution be completed with the complete dispossession of the capitalist class, the liberation of Spain's colonies, and the establishment of workers' power throughout the country. The Popular Front government should be replaced by a workers' state modelled on the Bolshevik regime of October 1917 in Russia. Those who reject this as unrealistic tend to forget that the Bolsheviks won their civil war, whereas the Popular Front government in Spain was defeated.

When Orwell arrived in Barcelona he found a city where "the working class was in the saddle", where the rich had fled or were in hiding and workers' control was the order of the day. In Britain, he had seen a working class that had still not recovered from defeat and betrayal, here he found a working class that had in Barcelona and elsewhere, seized power. This was worth fighting for. His enthusiasm still rings out of the pages of *Homage to Catalonia*. The book was and remains essential reading for anyone on the left. Orwell's experiences in revolutionary Barcelona changed his life forever. In Spain, he later wrote, he had "breathed the air of equality" and this was what socialism was all about. Not some sort of "planned state capitalism with the grab-motive left intact". For ordinary people, for the people he fought alongside, "Socialism means a classless society or it means nothing" (*Homage to Catalonia*, pp 18-19). Socialism was no longer something to be read about, discussed, theorised; he had actually seen it. He had seen the working class in power. The question of whether or not the working class could take power had been decisively settled once and for all. He was to never underestimate the obstacles in the way, but he was confident that democratic socialism, the complete expropriation of the rich and the establishment of workers' power was possible. In Marxist terms, whereas in Britain he had seen a 'class-in-itself', coping with exploitation and oppression, in Spain he saw a 'class-for-itself', a working class taking control, ending exploitation and oppression and dispossessing the rich. As he wrote home, "I have seen wonderful things and at last really believe in socialism, which I never did before" (CW 11, p 28).

ORWELL: *A Rebel's Guide*

★7:
MAY DAYS

Orwell fought in the POUM militia on the Catalan front. This was a quiet, secondary sector with the heaviest fighting taking place on the Madrid front where the International Brigades were heavily engaged. Orwell decided to transfer to the Brigades and this time he was accepted. He wanted to fight where it mattered most and he had been persuaded by the Communist argument that the revolution had to be put on hold until Franco was defeated. What he did not realise was that far from the revolution being put on hold, the Popular Front government, urged on by the Communists, was actually rolling back, liquidating the revolution. And alongside this, steps were being taken to prepare the destruction of the revolutionary left, starting with the POUM.

Orwell went on leave to Barcelona, preparatory to transferring to the International Brigades, only to find that the city had been transformed as working class power had been rolled back by the Communists. Once he had arrived in the city, the situation came to a head when the Communists took control of the telephone exchange, the last straw as far as the anarchists were concerned. They called a general strike and the barricades went up in what have become known as the May 1937 events. He threw his lot in with the anarchists and the POUM and against the Communists. For Orwell this led to another dramatic life-changing realisation. He somewhat belatedly recognised that the Communists were actively rolling back the revolution, restoring bourgeois normality, conciliating and reassuring the rich, and that this was all to do with the exigencies of Russian foreign policy. Far from the Communists being fighters for the international working class, for socialism, they were in reality fighters for the Stalin regime. Party leaders, propagandists and activists were prepared to lie about and cover up torture, murder and counter-revolution in defence of what was at that time the most brutal and murderous regime in the world. This was the second great lesson that Orwell learned in Spain.

The May events failed to defeat the Communists' rolling back of the revolution, and instead of joining the International Brigades, Orwell returned to the Catalan front line to once again fight alongside his ILP and POUM comrades. Here on 20 May, he was shot in the throat by a fascist sniper and sent back behind the lines for medical treatment. While he was recovering from his wound, the Popular Front government, once again at the instigation of the Communists, moved to proscribe the POUM, arrest its leaders and many activists and militants, condemning them for being in league with the fascists. Orwell himself only narrowly escaped arrest, going on the run. As far as the Communist secret police were concerned he and his wife Eileen were "known Trotskyists". Given his weakened condition, arrest would have meant almost certain death, either under interrogation or from medical neglect. The POUM leader, Andres Nin, a life-long socialist fighter, was arrested and then supposedly freed by fascist rescuers. In fact, he was secretly handed over to the Communist secret police who tortured him to death in an attempt to get him to confess to being a fascist agent. This was, of course, vehemently denied at the time, but is freely admitted today. Other revolutionaries were just disappeared, shot out of hand and disposed of, or were left to rot in Communist prisons, starved, brutalised, sometimes tortured to death or just left to die of neglect.

Orwell and Eileen escaped from Spain, and returned to Britain. He was determined to expose what was going on in Spain, to make the socialist movement aware of the counter-revolutionary role of the Stalinists. What he found, however, was that the Communist Party and its sympathisers had successfully convinced most of the left that the POUM was either in league with the fascists or was their dupe. Gollancz turned his proposed book about his Spanish experiences down unseen. The only people defending the POUM and exposing the role of the Communists in Spain seemed to be the ILP, indeed in many ways *Homage to Catalonia* can be usefully seen as an ILP book. Orwell's account did justice not just to his own experiences in Spain but to those of all the ILP volunteers, who had returned from the fighting to find themselves vilified as fascist agents or dupes, even finding their homes picketed by Communists denouncing their treachery.

Orwell's interpretation of events in Spain was replicated in the ILP press and other publications. One of the ILP's leaders, Fenner Brockway, for example, published a pamphlet in late 1937, *The Truth About Barcelona*, where he made the point that in May the POUM had tried to fulfil "the historic role which the Bolsheviks fulfilled in Moscow in 1917", while the "Communists took the part of the Mensheviks". And just as the Bolsheviks had been accused of being German agents in 1917, so were the POUM in 1937 but this time by the Communists! On 13 June 1938, Orwell joined the ILP.

Looking back in 1946, Orwell described how for him revolutionary Barcelona had "turned the scale and thereafter I knew where I stood". He went on: "Every serious line I have written since 1936 has been written, directly or indirectly, against totalitarianism and for democratic socialism" (CW 18, p 319). As far as he was concerned you had to take a side in the struggle, there was no alternative. The same holds true today.

★8:
INSIDE THE ILP

What was the politics that Orwell embraced at this time? He came back from Spain full of revolutionary fervour, very much on the far left politically and a determined opponent of Stalinism. As far as he was concerned, at this time, the way to overthrow capitalism in a country like Britain, involved a mass movement electing into office a real socialist government, not a Labour government half-heartedly committed to reforming the system, but a socialist government committed to abolishing the system altogether and immediately taking decisive strategic steps towards that end. This, he believed and he was certainly correct in this belief, would inevitably provoke resistance. The capitalist class would not allow themselves to be stripped of all their wealth and power without a fight. This was elementary as far as Orwell was concerned. The military coup in Spain and the rise of fascism throughout Europe showed how the capitalist class responded when it was seriously threatened. The working class had to be ready to respond to this by taking to the streets, by occupying the factories, the mines, the docks, the shops and the offices, disarming the military and the police, rounding up the capitalist class and their agents. It was the working class on the street and in the workplace who would establish workers' power. The election of a socialist majority in parliament would, he believed, start the revolutionary process off, but it would be completed by the working class taking power into their hands outside parliament. This was, of course, very much what had happened in Barcelona. He did not think there would necessarily be a civil war in Britain, or at least nothing as ferocious and bloody as was taking place in Spain, but ruling class resistance would certainly have to be put down by force if socialism was to be achieved. This was something he was absolutely certain of. He was to broadly adhere to this strategy for achieving socialism for the rest of his life.

While Orwell was very much part of the revolutionary current within the ILP, nevertheless he did not accept that building a revolutionary party was necessary if the struggle was to be successful. Partly this was a response to his experiences with Stalinism, both in Spain and back home in Britain, partly it was the influence that anarchist ideas had on him and partly it reflected his understanding of British politics and society where he did not believe a revolutionary party on the Bolshevik model would be either needed or useful. He put too much faith in spontaneity on its own being able to bring the system down without recognising the need for the most advanced sections of the working class to be organised to lead the mass movement in the struggle, not least in opposition to those urging moderation, restraint, compromise and even surrender both inside and outside parliament.

The other side of his rejection of the need for a revolutionary party was an underestimation of the need to combat reformism, to debate and argue with those who believed that the capitalist state could somehow be used to bring about socialism. History shows that these people either end up running the capitalist system in the interests of the capitalist class, calling on their supporters to make the sacrifices necessary for them to remain in power or being overthrown by sabotage or by force. Rather than having a parliamentary focus, a revolutionary party would be rooted in the day to day struggles of the class, developing the tactics and the strategies without which socialist victory would not be possible. It would have at the centre of its politics the recognition that the capitalist state could not be used to bring about socialism, but would have to be overthrown, smashed, if socialism was to be achieved. Nevertheless, Orwell's politics show quite clearly that he was on the side of revolution, however it was to come about. When the barricades went up, there could be no doubt about which side Orwell would have been on. This is something that many of his contemporary admirers even today would rather forget.

★9:
WAR AND
REVOLUTION

There have been numerous attempts made over the years to reduce Orwell to a Labourite, to a faithful loyal Labour Party supporter, certainly on the left of the Party, but nevertheless someone who saw Labourism as the way forward for the British working class and who was, moreover, content with the reforms of the 1945-51 Labour government. This is a complete travesty. It is another attempt to domesticate him, to defuse his revolutionary politics.

Orwell came back from Spain, as we have seen, very much on the far left, rejecting Labourism and looking to the development of a mass socialist movement. He absolutely rejected the calls for the establishment of a British Popular Front which were being made by the Communist Party and much of the Labour Left. As far as he was concerned a Popular Front strategy involved watering down socialist demands and lowering the level of working class struggle in order to build unity with Liberals and even Conservatives against the fascist menace. The consequences of this strategy were, as far as he was concerned, being realised in Spain. Instead, the class struggle had to be intensified. As he pointed out, the harsh reality was that while conditions in Nazi Germany were bad, conditions in many British colonies were actually worse at that time. He insisted, in an article that appeared in the *Adelphi* in July 1939 that the bulk of the proletariat exploited by the British capitalist class actually lived in the colonies. As bad as Nazi rule was for the German working class, Hitler had not yet been able "to make a penny an hour a normal industrial wage; it is perfectly normal in India, and we are at great pains to keep it so" (CW 11, p 360). He absolutely rejected the idea of allying with the people who exploited and oppressed India in order to fight Nazi Germany. When he wrote this, he was absolutely right, although the situation was to change once Nazi conquests delivered into their hands their own subject peoples to super exploit, enslave and indeed exterminate.

Orwell opposed what he saw as the drive towards war with the Nazis, a war not against fascism but rather a war to protect and expand the British Empire. He was never a pacifist, but rather saw himself as an anti-militarist. As far as he was concerned the use of force to defend imperialism had to be opposed, but the use of force in liberation struggles or to achieve socialism was perfectly legitimate. He maintained this stance up until the outbreak of war in September 1939. His opposition to war with Nazi Germany had first come under pressure when Stalin concluded his Pact with the Nazis in August 1939, effectively allying the two totalitarian dictatorships, which proceeded to divide Eastern Europe between them. He would have found it extremely difficult opposing war alongside the Communists. While he was to later argue that it was the "patriotism" that had been ingrained in his youth that in the end determined him to support the war, effectively breaking with the ILP and with many of his friends on the far left, he rationalised his change of position as involving recognition of having to sometimes be prepared to choose the lesser evil. This 'lesser evilism' was to recur as a theme in his thinking on a number of occasions as we shall see. What this did not involve, however, was any change in his advocacy of revolution.

Orwell looked at the war through Spanish glasses so to speak, arguing that the only way Britain was going to be able to defeat the Nazis was if there was a socialist revolution that swept away the corrupt old ruling class, put the working class in power, gave independence to the colonies and turned the war into a revolutionary war, raising the standard of socialist revolution throughout Europe. This was how the fascists could have been defeated in Spain and it was the only way the Nazis could be defeated today. Indeed, the task was actually made easier by the fact that the Communists had isolated themselves by their pro-Nazi stance rather than still peddling Popular Front illusions. His patriotism was a "Revolutionary Patriotism".

The Nazi conquest of Western Europe in the summer of 1940 left Britain isolated with the USA neutral and the Soviet Union still allied with the Nazis, indeed having joined in the attack on Poland the previous year and then having invaded Finland. Only a Britain transformed by socialist revolution had any chance of defeating the Nazis, and he believed this revolution was already getting underway. The protests against the selfishness of the "rich swine" in wartime London, preventing the use of the empty homes of the wealthy being used to rehouse bombed out working class families, showed that the city was coming to increasingly resemble "St Petersburg in 1916". As he wrote in the autumn of 1940,

"Only revolution can save England, that has been obvious for years, but now the revolution has started, and it may proceed quite quickly if only we can keep Hitler out". And this revolution would involve the complete expropriation of the ruling class so that "I dare say the London gutters will have to run with blood. All right let them if necessary". He looked forward to the day, not too far off, when "the red militias are billeted in the Ritz" (CW12, p 272). Needless to say, this was not and never has been the Labour Party's position!

★ 10:
THE LION AND
THE UNICORN

Orwell's main contribution to preparing for revolution was to edit a series of short books, the Searchlight series, presenting the case for revolutionary change, hoping to win over what he saw as the new middle class to the socialist cause. Ten volumes were published, costing 2 shillings (10p) each. The volumes that still most repay reading are Ritchie Calder's tremendous account of the Blitz from a class perspective, *The Lesson of London*, the *Daily Mirror* columnist William Connors' powerful indictment of class inequality and social privilege in wartime Britain, The English at War and Orwell's own *The Lion and the Unicorn*. In *The Lion and the Unicorn*, which was published in February 1941, he argues that a Bolshevik-style revolution is no longer possible in Britain, not least because of changes in the class structure and the increasing importance of white collar workers or as he puts it, the growth of the middle class, but he still completely rejects the Labour Party's "timid reformism". As far as he was concerned, the Labour Party supported both the capitalist system and British imperialism, with no sign that this was likely to change. And anyway, the capitalist state was completely in the hands of the Labour Party's "enemies", so even if it was elected into office, it always faced "the same dilemma... carry out your promises and risk revolt or continue with the same policy as the Conservatives, and stop talking about socialism". The Labour leadership just did not have the stomach for a serious fight with the ruling class. Their sole concern was with "drawing their salaries and periodically swapping jobs with the Conservatives". As far as he was concerned at this time, "Labour Party politics had become a variant of Conservatism".

What of *The Lion and the Unicorn*'s domestic political programme? In his text, Orwell refers at one point to Britain being a family with the wrong family members in charge. This cosy image has sometimes led to a failure to recognise the radicalism of the programme and anyway in how many families will some of those members currently in charge have to be shot, as Orwell warned was likely, in order to bring about necessary change? What Orwell proposed as the first steps towards a socialist Britain was the confiscation of the land, the coal mines, the banks and the major industries. This would decisively break the back of the capitalist class. The Stock Exchange would be pulled down. Private land ownership would be limited to fifteen acres in the countryside and prohibited altogether in the towns and cities. This would eliminate the likes of the Duke of Westminster, who at the time was a pro-Nazi antisemite multi-millionaire, hiding out in the House of Lords, and today, after no less than four Labour governments have held office and have at best only ever inconvenienced the capitalist class, is a twenty-eight year old multi-billionaire who effortlessly inherited his way to incredible wealth, influence and power. The great country houses would be turned into children's homes. And there would be a maximum income so that no one had more than ten times the minimum income to live on. Private education would be abolished with Harrow, Eton and the rest of them nationalised, turned into comprehensive schools. He did propose keeping a constitutional monarchy although where he would have found a member of the royal family prepared to go along with all this is anybody's guess. And this was just the beginning.

The new socialist movement that would be necessary to carry out this programme would have the members of the trade unions and of what he hoped would be the defunct Labour Party at its core but it would also rally "most of the middle class… skilled workers, technical experts, airmen, scientists, architects and journalists". In *The Lion and the Unicorn*, he did not think that bloodshed was inevitable but if the capitalist class resisted its overthrow, the new socialist government would have to "shoot traitors" and as for an attempted coup, it "would crush any open revolt promptly and cruelly". This was, of course, one of the lessons he drew from Spain (CW12, pp 392-434).

Orwell's often celebrated discussion of Englishness in *The Lion and the Unicorn* was very much part of an attempt on his part at making revolutionary politics acceptable to a patriotic middle class readership. It needs to be put very firmly in context. At around the same time as the publication of the book, the Left Book Club, which had decisively broken with the Communists after the Russian invasion of Finland, published an article by Orwell, 'Fascism and Democracy' in its magazine, *Left News*. Here he was addressing a committed leftwing audience so no protracted celebration of Englishness was necessary. He considered the limitations of bourgeois democracy. It was "negatived by economic inequality", people get to vote once every five years, but the rest of the time the working man's life is "dictated by his employer" and "most important of all, nearly the whole cultural and intellectual life of the community – newspapers, books, education, films, radio – is controlled by monied men who have the strongest motive to prevent the spread of certain ideas". Indeed, in the bourgeois democracies, people are "'conditioned' from birth onwards". And if by some chance a government representing working people was elected into office and proved too radical, "the rich can usually blackmail it by threatening to export capital" and if that did not work, "the monied classes would rebel and probably with success because they would have most of the permanent officials and the key men in the armed forces on their side". As he summed up, and this was a point he continually returned to in his political writings: "There is no strong reason for thinking that any really fundamental change can ever be achieved peacefully". Nevertheless, he insisted, quite correctly, that the civil liberties that ordinary people had fought for under bourgeois democracy were of crucial importance and had to be vigorously defended and indeed extended under socialism. When the new socialist movement emerged, he wrote, it would be "both revolutionary and democratic. It will aim at the most fundamental changes and be perfectly willing to use violence if necessary" (CW12, pp 376-381). Another article, 'Our Opportunity', published in *Left News* in January 1941, actually proclaimed that "the feeling of all true patriots and all true socialists is at bottom reducible to the Trotskyist slogan: 'The war and the revolution are inseparable'" (CW12, pp 345-346). Both articles were republished in a volume edited by Gollancz, *The Betrayal of the Left*.

11:
THE RULING
CLASS HOLD ON

None of this came to pass of course. While Orwell can certainly be seen as having misjudged, indeed exaggerated, the potential for radicalisation in 1940-41, he was absolutely right in his later judgement that the British capitalist class had been saved from defeat – his alternative to socialist revolution – by the Nazi attack on the Soviet Union and by the Japanese attack on the United States. Stalin and Roosevelt came to their rescue. A good indication that he was having doubts about socialist revolution being imminent was his decision in the summer of 1941 to go and work at the BBC, essentially as a propagandist. He only really finally accepted that the opportunity for the emergence of a new socialist movement had passed, however, when the Churchill coalition government set about crushing the Congress movement in India without it provoking any great protest in Britain. In August 1942, the British arrested Gandhi, banned the Congress movement and put down the resulting 'Quit India' revolt by means of brutal repression. Not only was this wholeheartedly supported by the Labour ministers in the coalition but the crackdown was actually ordered, not by Churchill who was out of the country at the time, but by the Deputy Prime Minister, Clement Attlee, the leader of the Labour Party. Villages were burned down, protesting crowds were machine gunned from the air, hundreds of women were raped by police and troops, prisoners were publicly flogged and summarily executed, and more than 10,000 people were killed by government forces. There were over 90,000 arrests with prisoners routinely mistreated, beaten, starved, denied sleep for days, even forced to eat excreta.

Orwell was both appalled and disgusted by the repression that was unleashed in India. As far as he was concerned it showed that the reactionaries were securely in the saddle domestically and that the opportunity to overthrow the British ruling class had passed. Despite this, he continued to support the British war effort on the principle that British imperialism, for all its crimes, was the still the lesser evil.

One important article that he wrote some time in 1942, 'Looking Back on the Spanish Civil War', captures his thinking as he reluctantly realised that there was not going to be a socialist revolution in the immediate future and wrestled with the consequences. Here he lamented the failure of the international working class to overthrow capitalism, but still argued a powerful defence of working people, struggling for "enough to eat, freedom from the haunting terror of unemployment… and short enough working hours to leave you with a little energy when the day is done". He insisted that "the working class will go on struggling against fascism after the others have caved in". The working class might be "blind and stupid", an unfortunate choice of words to say the least, although he meant kept in the dark and kept ignorant, but, he insisted, "it knows enough to keep pushing towards the light and it will do this in the face of endless discouragement". He concluded that despite his support for the war involving degrading himself to "the equivocal moral position of Britain", with its "democratic phrases" and its empire based on virtual slavery, he still believed that the war was at bottom about whether or not ordinary people could live "the decent fully human life which is now technically attainable… Shall the common man be pushed back in the mud, or shall he not?" He still insisted that "the common man will win his fight sooner or later, but I want it to be sooner and not later – some time within the next hundred years say… That was the real issue of the Spanish War, and of the present war and of other wars still to come" (CW13, pp 509-510). Within the next hundred years gives us until 2042!

Orwell was to leave the BBC in November 1943, at least in part because of increasing censorship. He hoped that as far as possible, he had "kept our little corner of it fairly clean" (CW14, p214). Nevertheless, he complained to one of his friends that working for the Corporation was like being "an orange that's been trodden on by a very dirty boot" (CW15, pp 306). One cannot help feeling that this would have been a more appropriate, a more honest, statue, an orange being trodden on by a dirty boot, to be erected in his honour outside the BBC than what was actually put in place!

★12:
THE AMERICAN
CONNECTION

When he left the BBC, he went to work at the *Tribune* newspaper as literary editor. *Tribune* was the paper of the dissident Labour left, edited by Aneurin Bevan MP. It was fiercely opposed to the policies of the Churchill coalition government, not sparing its Labour ministers. In its literary pages, Orwell gave a voice at various times to just about everyone on the dissident left, anarchists, ILP members, Trotskyists, non-affiliated socialists, indeed to everyone except the Stalinists. And why not? He never joined the Labour Party and the Stalinists had tried to kill him after all. What is important to recognise though is that most of his political writing was never published in *Tribune*. Since early 1941 he had written a regular 'London Letter', chronicling the British Home Front, for the far left US journal, *Partisan Review*. He contributed fifteen of these up until his last in the summer of 1946. The significance of this is often missed in discussions of Orwell's politics, but the fact that most of his political writing between 1941 and 1946 appeared in the pages of what was still a journal heavily influenced by Trotskyist ideas is of considerable importance.

Although he worked for *Tribune*, he was not a Labourite. This has to be insisted on. In Britain, Trotskyism had never established itself as an intellectual force in the way that it had in the United States so that there was no British equivalent of *Partisan Review*.

If there had been then Orwell would certainly have been involved with it and his intellectual biography would look different with his involvement with *Tribune* relegated to its proper place. Indeed, throughout the rest of his life, Orwell was to maintain a continual dialogue with anarchist and Trotskyist ideas, and, in fact these ideas were, as we shall see, central to his two best known novels, *Animal Farm* and *Nineteen Eighty Four*.

It is in *Partisan Review* that we can best follow the development of his political thinking. In the March-April 1943 issue of the magazine, he wrote of how while the military situation was improving, "the political situation is blacker than it has ever been". He went on: "the forces of reaction have won hands down... we may all have underrated the strength of capitalism". One indication of the shift to the right that he identified was the enthusiasm with which the Beveridge *Report on Social Security* had been welcomed. What he described as "a very modest measure of reform" was, of course, to become one of the foundations of the reform programme of the Labour government elected in 1945 (CW14, pp292-293). As far as Orwell was concerned, the Report in no way threatened the wealth and power of the capitalist class, far from it, and had nothing to do with socialism, sentiments that William Beveridge, a Liberal, would have wholeheartedly agreed with! It ameliorated rather than overthrew the capitalist system.

One question worth considering is whether or not the Second World War was in any way a 'People's War'? Not as far as Orwell was concerned. How could it be? The country was still securely in the hands of the ruling class. Early in 1944, he dismissed the idea that

Britain was "democratic, if by democracy, you meant 'popular rule'". A more accurate description was that Britain was "a plutocracy haunted by a caste system", a description that remains depressingly true to this day (CW16, p67). He certainly did not underestimate the importance of civil liberties as he have seen, but as far as recognising where power was actually concentrated, it was in the hands of the rich and their agents. Later that year, he was to write that there had been some changes brought about by the demands of the war effort, so that the country had moved in the direction of a planned economy and there had been some lessening in class distinction, but, he still insisted that "the same people still own all the property and usurp all the best jobs" (CW16, p 412). What was the way forward?

★13:
THE LABOUR
GOVERNMENT

With hopes for the emergence of a new socialist movement remaining unfulfilled, Orwell
came round to regarding the Labour Party
as the best that could be hoped for in the circumstances.
Even though it was not a socialist party, a Labour government would be the lesser evil. Undoubtedly, Attlee's
invitation to Aneurin Bevan to join the government
led to Orwell expecting more radicalism, measures
that would seriously threaten the capitalist class, and
indeed, this has been the historic role of the Labour Left,
convincing members and supporters that Labour government's are going to be more radical than they ever
really are. In August 1945, he told *Partisan Review* readers that if the Labour government meant business then
it would immediately "nationalise land, coal mines,
railways, public utilities and banks", offer "India immediate Dominium Status (this is a minimum)" and begin
a purge of the senior echelons of the civil service and the
military "so thoroughly as to forestall sabotage from the
right". If this was not done then "it is a good bet that no
really radical economic change is intended" (CW17,pp
339-340). He was speedily disillusioned.

When he tried to use the pages of *Tribune* to express
his dissatisfaction with a proposed article calling on
the government to urgently abolish the House of Lords
and the public schools, it was made clear to him that
this sort of criticism was no longer acceptable. He

became increasingly disillusioned with *Tribune*, not least because of the paper's strong support for Zionism, which he considered to be just another example of European colonialism, displacing the Palestinians with European settlers. Instead, Orwell called for 100,000 Jewish refugees to be allowed into Britain. His opposition to Zionism led inevitably to him being accused of antisemitism. The Labour government's policy at this time was quite shamefully, as far as possible, to keep Holocaust survivors out of the country even while at the very same time recruiting workers from Eastern Europe to meet a chronic post-war shortage of labour. Most notoriously a surrendered Ukrainian SS Division was allowed into the country to settle en masse!

In his last 'London Letter' in *Partisan Review* that appeared in the summer of 1946, he complained about "how little change seems to have happened as yet in the structure of society". He welcomed the nationalisation of the railways, but observed that the "shareholders are being bought out at prices they would hardly get in the open market". As far as "the social set-up" was concerned "there is no symptom by which one could infer we are not living under a Conservative government". The House of Lords was still in existence, there had been no visible effort to "democratise education", and no purge of the civil service or the military. He went on: "the upper classes are still living their accustomed life, and though they certainly dislike the Labour government, they don't appear to be frightened of it" (CW18, p28). What this demonstrates, of course, is his failure to understand the nature of Labour reformism. There was no way the future Viscount Attlee, who was, of course, a former public schoolboy himself and a great admirer of the public school system, was going to abolish either the House of Lords or the public schools. The very idea was unthinkable. Labour's welfare reforms, most notably the creation of the NHS, were intended to and indeed did ameliorate the condition of the working class, improve the conditions under which they were exploited. They were not intended to end their exploitation or to overthrow the British class system, to put an end to the British ruling class. And Labour's nationalisation measures were certainly not intended to overthrow British capitalism, but rather to help modernise it, to strengthen it. Of course, the ruling class objected to any coddling of the working class, with the King of all people complaining to the Labour Chancellor of the Exchequer about the common people getting free medical treatment, but their wealth, privilege and power was all left intact. The British class system remained essentially unchanged, but the position of the working class, while still very much that of a subordinate class, was improved.

Orwell was particularly worried about the Labour government's attitude towards the British Empire. The use of British troops to restore French rule in Indo-China and Dutch rule in Indonesia, both involving heavy fighting, by the Labour government certainly showed that these fears were well-grounded. In November 1945, writing in another far left US journal, *Commentary*, he insisted that "Britain cannot become a genuinely socialist country while continuing to plunder Asia and Africa" (CW17, p340). In fact, the Labour government was determined to keep as much of the

British Empire as possible under British control and to intensify the exploitation of the colonies. This was necessary if Britain was to maintain its great power status. British policy provoked a Communist insurrection in Malaya in 1948 and the Mau Mau rebellion in Kenya in 1952 although this only broke out after Labour had lost power. As for the withdrawal from India, this took place not because of any non-existent Labour commitment to support national liberation struggles. Far from it! The government hoped to hand over power to a weak puppet government that it could continue to dominate after independence, with British military bases remaining in the country and Indian troops still being available to fight for the Empire. Instead the growing unrest in the country forced a precipitate withdrawal that has been subsequently dressed up as a great act of liberal statesmanship. This is one of the great myths of British Labourism. Indeed, Clement Attlee has actually been celebrated as the liberator of India! He was no such thing. The very fact that there was no serious backlash in Britain against Indian independence showed that the ruling class as a whole, including the senior generals, recognised the country could no longer be held by force and that withdrawal was necessary.

Given his disillusionment, why did Orwell continue to support the Labour government, with whatever reservations, right up until his death? It was the beginning of the Cold War that convinced him that the government had to be supported no matter what, that the alternatives were too dangerous, even threatening the country's very survival. It was yet another lesser evil.

★14: THE COLD WAR

The Hitler-Stalin Pact had seriously damaged the credibility of both the British Communist Party and the Soviet Union on the left. With the Nazi attack on the Soviet Union in June 1941, this began to change. The ferocity of the fighting on the Eastern Front, the enormous casualties, both civilian and military, suffered by the Soviet Union, and the role the Red Army played in turning the tide all combined to turn Stalin into something of a popular hero, 'Uncle Joe', and to erase the memory of the Great Terror and of the Pact. The revival of sympathy for the Soviet Union on the British left was of considerable concern to Orwell. His worries were not just informed by his experiences in Spain, but ever since his return home from that conflict, he had read widely on the Soviet Union and had concluded that the murderous regime that held power had nothing whatsoever to do with socialism. He had first considered that it might be a kind of state capitalism, but had eventually settled on the notion that it was an entirely new kind of exploitative system, a system where a new bureaucratic ruling class controlled a collectivised economy in its own interests, exercising power without any restraint. This was the theory of bureaucratic collectivism, which he was introduced to at least partly through the agency of *Partisan Review*. It was the theory associated with a breakaway faction of US Trotskyists led by Max Schachtman. They had broken with Trotsky who right up until his assassination in August 1940 had still argued that the Soviet

Union was some sort of workers' state, a workers' state that had degenerated but that still had to be given support. As far as the dissident Trotskyists were concerned the Soviet Union had nothing whatsoever to do with socialism and indeed the workers were worse off than under capitalism. As for Orwell, he regarded the revival of sympathy for the Communists and the Soviet Union as a serious threat to the prospects for building a genuine socialist movement in Britain. It was this that prompted him to write *Animal Farm*.

★15: THE REVOLUTION BETRAYED

Animal Farm told the story of the Russian Revolution and of the Stalin regime's coming to power in the form of a fable, of a farm animals' revolt against the farmer. It was, in his words, an exploration of "Marx's theory from the animals' point of view… that men exploit animals in much the same way as the rich exploit the proletariat" (CW19, p 88). It was also very much informed by both the Trotskyist notion of the Revolution having been betrayed and by the anarchist belief that this betrayal had occurred as early as the Kronstadt Rising of 1921. At the time, it was a massive slap in the face for the growing number of apologists for the Stalin regime on the left. It is sometimes argued that the book repudiated the very idea of revolution. This is not true. It did not condemn revolution, far from it, but rather the betrayal of the revolution. Orwell himself made this clear when he wrote to an American Trotskyist friend, Dwight Macdonald, emphasising that "I meant the moral to be that revolutions only effect a radical improvement when the masses are alert and know how to chuck out their leaders as soon as the latter have done their job". There was no such thing, he insisted, as "a benevolent dictatorship" and that you can't have a revolution "unless you make it for yourself" (CW18, p 507). He certainly believed that the Bolshevik party model of organisation had facilitated the rise to power of Stalin. What is also important as far as placing the book in context is concerned, is that at the time he wrote it, he intended to show that the pigs' regime was as bad as that of the farmers, that it was just as reactionary and that, in the end, you could not, as he put it, tell the pigs from the men. The Soviet Union was as bad as imperial Britain and the capitalist United States. It was not progressive, but behaved like every other great state and ruthlessly and brutally exploited and oppressed the mass of its population. By the time he came to write *Nineteen Eighty Four*, he had shifted ground in response to the Cold War so that Big Brother's regime was now far worse than Attlee's Britain or Truman's USA.

At the end of the Second World War though, Orwell had not yet embraced the concerns of the Cold War. He condemned British intervention in Greece to crush the Communist-led Greek resistance that began in 1944. This had been initiated under the coalition government with Labour support and was then continued by the Labour government. As far as Orwell was concerned, you could not legitimately condemn Russian intervention against the Polish resistance and support British intervention against the Greek resistance. He even supported the Greek Communists' right to fight back against the British. On another occasion, towards the end of 1945, he refused to support the League of European Freedom in its opposition to the Russian takeover of Eastern Europe because it did not condemn British rule in India. And Orwell involved himself at this time in a little known campaign organised by the British Trotskyist organisation, the Revolutionary Communist Party, demanding that the Allied war crimes investigators look into the validity of the confessions made at the Moscow Trials by Stalin's victims. Many of the leaders of the Russian Revolution had confessed that they, together with Trotsky, were working for the Nazis in the 1930s. Indeed Trotsky was even supposed to have had a secret meeting with Rudolf Hess, Hitler's deputy! All this supposedly took place before the Hitler-Stalin Pact of course. With German records now in Allied hands, these confessions could at last be definitively proven to be lies, extracted by intimidation, threats to family members and torture. He urged the secretary of the Revolutionary Communist Party, W Wood, to try and get more signatures for their petition, suggesting people they could usefully approach. The campaign failed, although it does seem to have caused the Labour government some concern that it might compromise relations with the Soviet Union.

Orwell made his position at this time absolutely clear in a 'Preface' that he wrote for a Ukrainian edition of *Animal Farm* in March 1947. Here he forcefully argued that the "Soviet myth" had a "negative influence… on the western socialist movement" and that "it was of the utmost importance to me that people in western Europe should see the Soviet regime for what it really was". As far as he was concerned nothing had done so much to corrupt "the original idea of socialism as the belief that Russia is a socialist country". For Orwell, the destruction of the "Soviet myth was essential if we want a revival of the socialist movement" (CW 19, p 88). His commitment to the struggle for socialism and to the overthrow of capitalism was absolute.

★16: NINETEEN EIGHTY FOUR

By the time Orwell came to write *Nineteen Eighty Four*, he had come to the conclusion that war between Britain and the USA on one side and the Soviet Union on the other was more or less inevitable. He was still wrestling with the implications of this, but was increasingly coming round to the idea that Britain and the USA were the lesser evil and would have to be supported. Certainly, the portrayal of Big Brother's totalitarian regime reflects this. *Nineteen Eighty Four* shows a society completely dominated by a tyrannical state that can even change facts if it so chooses, most famously 2+2=5. Surveillance is total, informing on friends and family all pervasive and the regime can effortlessly manipulate a population that has been reduced to complete docility… except for the proles. The proles are controlled by the sort of methods that Orwell regarded as those being used to control the working class in his own time. Consequently they have retained their humanity, their loyalty to each other even if they have been prevented from imagining a socialist future. Because the book was to become an important propaganda weapon in the Cold War, this dimension, that if there was any hope it lay with the proles, was generally ignored, dismissed. It still is today. The sentiment was obviously of no account because it contradicted the Cold War discourse within which the novel had become situated both in Britain and the United States. Indeed, the book was used to attack both socialism and communism. This had started even before Orwell's death. It was certainly not his intention that it should be used in this way and he was already starting to try and counteract this in his last days. In July 1949, he actually wrote to correspondents in the USA that the book was "NOT INTENDED as an attack on socialism" (CW19, p 88). The capital letters clearly indicate that he was aware of the difficulty of getting this point across. Certainly, his early death, cutting short his protests, was an important factor in allowing the right to effectively confiscate the book, but equally important was that so much of the left was still sympathetic to the Soviet Union, turning a blind eye to the police states being installed across Eastern Europe, apologising for the so-called Titoite purges, effectively handing the book over to the right at this time.

What Orwell does in *Nineteen Eighty Four* is show his readers a monstrous tyranny that derives from both Nazism and Stalinism as seen through the perspective of the theory of *bureaucratic collectivism or oligarchic collectivism* as it is called in the novel. It is an attack on Stalinism from the left not the right and there is, it has to be insisted, nothing in the book that can be seriously seen as unfair to the either the regime in the Soviet Union or its various puppet regimes throughout Eastern Europe. The book's protagonist, Winston Smith, is convinced that it is only the proles who can overthrow Big Brother, but he confronts the dilemma that Orwell himself had confronted since the late 1930s and that all socialists have to confront: if socialism is so obviously the solution, why hasn't the working class taken up the cause and brought the system down? This was the question he had first asked when he visited the North of England in 1936, that he thought had been answered in Spain, but that he found himself asking again and again throughout the 1940s. As Winston Smith puts it: "Until they become conscious they will never rebel, and until after they have rebelled they cannot become conscious". This certainly does not indicate any abandonment of the socialist cause on Orwell's part, but rather the exploration of an understandable doubt, but a doubt that is nevertheless resolved. Winston Smith remains committed to his belief in the agency of the proles up until his arrest. Indeed, he actually gives voice to one of the most powerful statements of socialist hope and commitment in English fiction, a statement that once again is generally overlooked at least initially because of the domination of Cold War concerns. He is watching a working class woman hanging out the washing and recognises that "everywhere, all over the world, hundreds of thousands of millions of people just like this, people ignorant of one another's existence, held apart by walls of hatred and lies, and yet almost exactly the same – people who had never learned to think but who were storing up in their hearts and bellies and muscles the power that would one day overturn the world". Such working class women in London and New York, Paris and Berlin, Russia, Africa, Brazil, China and Japan, were "unconquerable... made monstrous by work and child-bearing, toiling from birth to death and still singing. Out of those loins a race of conscious beings must one day come" (NEF, pp74, 229-230). And then the game would be up for the ruling class everywhere.

★ 17:
LAST DAYS

O rwell continued to support the Labour government even after he had given up any hope that
it might move the country in the direction of
socialism. The main reason for this was the Cold War.
He believed that the Labour government was the best
defence against the Soviet Union, not least because it
would be able to persuade the working class to make
the necessary sacrifices. A Conservative government
demanding the same sacrifices would only plunge the
country into class conflict and this would play into the
hands of the Communist Party. And when the Labour
government did impose austerity, including the first
ever cuts to the NHS, in the pursuit of a massive rearma-
ment programme, he supported it, even when it began
using troops to break strikes. What was at stake was
the very survival of the country as far as he was concerned. His support for the Labour government right or
wrong pulled him to the right, as it has done many on
the Labour Left over the years, and saw him supporting
policies and actions that he would have wholeheartedly
opposed if carried out by any other government. Once
again, this can be seen as a consequence of his failure
to really get to grips with Labour reformism and its
consequences.

It was also his support for the Labour government
that led him into his relationship with the black propaganda outfit, the Information Research Department
(IRD) that the government had set up to carry on the

propaganda war against the Communists. From the very beginning, the IRD set about recruiting people on the left politically who were also anti-Stalinist. As for Orwell, he provided them with a list of people who were not reliable anti-Stalinists. This has been fastened on by many Stalinist sympathisers as showing him up as an informer, a supporter of a British McCarthyism. Certainly he made a serious mistake becoming involved with the IRD, but there is something unsavoury about those who clung to the certainties of Stalinism, turning a blind eye to mass murder and slave labour camps actually criticising Orwell. And, indeed, at the very same time, Orwell was an active opponent of any restriction of civil liberties by the Labour government including those of Communist Party members. He was actively involved in the Freedom Defence Committee that had been established as a libertarian alternative to the National Council of Civil Liberties which was under Communist Party control and had refused to defend the civil liberties of anarchists and Trotskyists.

Even while he was writing *Nineteen Eighty Four*, even while he was assisting the IRD, Orwell was still critically engaging with the ideas of the far left. What we can see here is that Orwell was grappling with difficult times, often making mistakes, bad mistakes, but still remaining wholeheartedly committed to democratic socialism. In the July-August 1947 issue of *Partisan Review*, he published an article, 'On European Unity' as part of a series on 'The Future of Socialism'. This was his last fully worked out political statement. The first point to make is that nowhere in the article does he recommend Labourism and the Labour government as having anything to do with a socialist future! Instead of celebrating the Labour government, he wrote that "a socialist today is in the position of a doctor treating an all but hopeless case". Hardly a ringing endorsement of British Labourism! Nevertheless, as a socialist, he recognised that you had to believe "that socialism can be established". He outlined what he thought were the terrible dangers facing humanity, concluding that the only way to avoid these dangers was if "democratic socialism" was "made to work throughout some large area". He thought Western Europe the most likely prospect, although he acknowledged that "socialism cannot properly be said to be established until it is world-wide, but the process must begin somewhere". There was the opposition of the Soviet Union and its puppet Communist Parties to be overcome. Too many workers still believed in 'the Russian myth' especially in Europe. There was the hostility of the United States which was a particular problem because Britain was "almost a dependency of the USA". The only way to break this dependency was for Britain to give up "its attempt to be an extra-European power". Britain and the other European powers had to liberate their empires: "the European nations must stop being exploiters abroad if they are to build true socialism at home". He thought it most unlikely that this could be accomplished "without bloodshed". In particular, Britain had to "get out of India". He did not rule out the prospect of the Russian people overthrowing Stalinism. This was when he was writing *Nineteen Eighty Four*, which should remind us that it was a novel and not a manifesto. Nor did he rule out the development of a mass socialist movement in the United States some time in the future. As far as he was concerned though, "the only worth-while political objective today" was "a socialist United States of Europe" (CW19, pp163-167). This would, he insisted, be only the first step towards a socialist world. Orwell was very much an International Socialist.

Orwell died on 21 January 1950, complaining to the last about the timidity of the Labour government. He told Stephen Spender from his hospital bed that he had expected more than "the Beveridge Plan and Welfare State", indeed, he had hoped for a "manifest revolution". Instead, there were "far too many visible signs of wealth in London... all these Rolls Royces" (Newsinger, *Hope Lies in the Proles*, p 135). If he had lived into the 1950s, would he have supported the Korean War with its terrible toll in civilian dead or would he have responded as he had to British intervention in Greece? We have no way of knowing. We can feel absolutely confident he would have opposed the joint British, French and Israeli invasion of Egypt, the Suez invasion in 1956, and that he would have supported the Hungarian rising against Soviet domination that same year. The working class in Hungary set up workers' councils and established a system of dual power that was only suppressed by the intervention of Russian tanks. Working class districts were shelled as 200,000 Russian troops occupied the country. The Hungarian workers responded with a protracted general strike that led the Communist regime to make inciting strikes a capital offence! There can be little doubt whose side he would have been on here. But back home, would he have supported the Campaign for Nuclear Disarmament (CND)? We don't know. Once again, we can really have no idea about how his ideas would have developed if he had survived into the 1950s, the 1960s, even the 1970s. Would he have remained a socialist or would he have gone over to the right? Would he have given up his longstanding identification with the poor and the oppressed, with the working class, and gone over to the side of their exploiters and oppressors? The answer generally tells us more about the person offering the opinion than it does about Orwell, often reflecting their own trajectory. What we can be certain of though, is that once he came home from Spain, he remained a democratic socialist, committed to fighting for the overthrow of capitalism worldwide by force if necessary right up until his death.

.

FURTHER READING

The best biography of Orwell remains Bernard Crick's *George Orwell* (1992), but also Gordon Bowker's *George Orwell* (2003).

For more on Orwell's socialism see my *Orwell's Politics* (1999) and *Hope Lies in the Proles: George Orwell and the Left* (2018).

Orwell's own writings have been collected in his invaluable *Complete Works*, edited by Peter Davison and there are many *Selected Collections* in print as well.

His books including *Down and Out in Paris and London*, *The Road to Wigan Pier*, *Homage to Catalonia*, *Animal Farm* and *Nineteen Eighty Four* are all in print.

All are available from Bookmarks: The Socialist Bookshop
www.bookmarksbookshop.co.uk